A BROADS-EYE VIEW 2

MORE AERIAL PHOTOGRAPHS OF THE NORFOLK AND SUFFOLK BROADS

MIKE PAGE & PAULINE YOUNG

HALSGROVE

First published in Great Britain in 2008
Reprinted 2009

Title page: **Hoveton Great Broad**

Access to the Broad is from the river only. The most spectacular time to visit is when the terns are nesting. A platform has been placed out on the broad and the terns can be watched from one of the hides. Along the 1km boardwalk there are information boards and at one point there's a pole and an invitation to see just how far into the soft mud the pole can be pushed. It's alarming. Salhouse Broad is to the left of picture with Wroxham Broad top centre.

British Library Cataloguing-in-Publication Data
A CIP record for this title is available from the British Library

ISBN 978 1 84114 704 8

HALSGROVE
Halsgrove House,
Ryelands Industrial Estate,
Bagley Road, Wellington, Somerset TA21 9PZ
Tel: 01823 653777   Fax: 01823 216796
email: sales@halsgrove.com

Part of the Halsgrove group of companies
Information on all Halsgrove titles is available at: www.halsgrove.com

Printed and bound by Grafiche Flaminia, Italy

CONTENTS

Tangmere **crosses the Yare at Lakenham**

ACKNOWLEDGEMENTS

Mike Page would like to thank his co-pilots from Seething Airfield: Brian Barr, Peter Day, Tim Ball, Jonathan Howes and Gerry Parsons. And everyone at Norwich Air Traffic Control for their good-humoured help and cooperation.

Pauline Young would like to thank especially Alison Yardy, Richard Adderson and Robert Malster, but also Dr Pam Taylor, Canon Geoffrey Tarris, Robert Young, Kevin Taylor, Peter Bower, Christine Richardson and Jamie Campbell. And Judy Speed for her meticulous proof reading.

And with this, our fourth book, we once again thank our spouses Gillian Page and John Young for their forbearance with our preoccupations whilst this book was in preparation. Special thanks also to Roy Snelling without whom none of these books would have been possible.

Mike Page, Strumpshaw
Pauline Young, Wymondham
2008

FOREWORD

The Norfolk and Suffolk Broads are one of Britain's most sensitive and complex areas of out-standing beauty.   Michael Page's brilliant aerial pictures have captured these components and characteristics, together with the region's moods, in an altogether delightful style.   Since the earlier book *A Broads Eye View* much work has taken place on flood alleviation provision and this too is well illustrated.

You will really enjoy these superb birds'-eye views of The Broads together with Pauline Young's well-researched accompanying explanatory commentary.

James Hoseason OBE
Beccles Autumn 2007

Belaugh

Upton Boat Dyke

This book is dedicated to Mike's friend Robin Scriven of Norwich Air Traffic Control. Robin died suddenly during 2007 and will be greatly missed.

We'd like also to add a dedication to the youngest members of our respective families: Tyler Robinson, Mia Page Robinson, Jonathan Page, Patrick Page and Sophie Julia Young, in the hope that they too, as they grow up, will develop a love of The Broads.

INTRODUCTION

Since *A Broads-Eye View* was published in 2005 there have been many changes in Broadland. The changes mainly relate to the vast amount of work being done to alleviate flooding in vulnerable areas. This in turn has changed the landscape and it's far easier to see from the air than it is on the ground. Water quality overall has improved too and this again can be well demonstrated from a height of five hundred feet or more, especially in the treated areas. All of this you will find in *A Broads-Eye View 2* together with areas not filmed for our first book. Mike Page has begun at the source of each river and flown along its entire length resulting in some altogether new pictures. Pauline Young has interpreted those pictures and on occasion has added extra detail or anecdotes to bring them even more to life.

As with the other three books of aerial pictures, all royalties received will go to a local charity.

Mike Page, Strumpshaw
Pauline Young, Wymondham
2008

Mautby Marsh Mill

RIVER BURE

At just over 30 miles the River Bure, or the 'North River', is the longest navigable river in Broadland. The word may be a corruption of Burgh, old English for a fort – a few miles downstream from its source is the village of Burgh next Aylsham through which the Bure flows. In common with the River Ant there was canalisation of the upper reaches to create the Aylsham navigation (1774). Today the river flows into the Yare at Great Yarmouth and thence into the North Sea but centuries earlier it discharged further north at Grubb's Haven, known also as Cockle Water, near Caister.

The source of the Bure

Melton Constable is better known for its early railway associations ('the Crewe of East Anglia') rather than as the source of the River Bure. The village was the hub of the M&GN (Midland and Great Northern Railway) and by 1887 lines ran northwards to Holt and Cromer, south to Norwich, west to King's Lynn and The Midlands and east to Great Yarmouth. Nothing remains of all this activity except for the tell tale curved line (middle distance) which is the 'fossilised' track of the old M&GN line to Norwich City Station. In the foreground is the site of the locomotive works (also now gone).

Saxthorpe and Corpusty Mill

The present mill was built at the end of the seventeenth century. The river is the parish boundary so there was a situation here where grain was taken in on the Saxthorpe side and flour or feed delivered from Corpusty! The mill was referred to as Saxthorpe or Corpusty Mill depending on which side of the river you lived. The previous mill was built for fulling (washing) wool, an important industry from the Middle Ages onwards for several centuries.

Corpusty's name possibly has its origins as being the pigsty (or stig) of one Mr Corp who lived at least a thousand years ago. The Midland and Great Northern Railway reached Corpusty in 1883. In 1888 the journey to Norwich by train involved a change at Melton Constable, the whole trip taking fifty-five minutes, there were at least three trains a day. In 1932 the Eastern Counties Omnibus Service ran twice a day from Saxthorpe to Norwich, the journey taking one hour. Today an independent coach company runs several services a day between Corpusty and Norwich but still the journey takes between forty and fifty minutes depending on the time of day. Not much change there then in over a century!

Itteringham

The parish of Itteringham in 1088 was a gift from William the Conqueror to William de Warrene for his earlier support at the Battle of Hastings. It didn't do him much good though, he died from an arrow wound the same year. Modernity caught up with Itteringham when it became on the stage coach route in the eighteenth century. The Holt to Norwich coach passed through the village three times a week. The mill, hidden in the trees, keeps pace with energy needs and supplies electricity by micro-hydroturbine into the National Grid.

The Blickling Estate

The River Bure meanders past what is considered to be one of the National Trust's 'Jewels in the Crown'. The Jacobean house was built for Sir Henry Hobart Lord Chief Justice during the reign of James I. It was begun in 1616. It's a surprise suddenly to come upon this magnificent house from the public road. The fifteen feet wide yew hedges flanking the approach were planted probably in the eighteenth century. The parterre formal gardens to the right of the hall are a 1930s adaptation of a Victorian design. Although the church predates the Hall much of what we see today is Victorian.

Ingworth looking upriver

Several hundred years ago the river was altered to allow the mill to be built nearer the village, the earlier course is to the left of the picture. The mill ceased working in 1912 and was dismantled. Described as a 'half mill' it meant that two owners shared the profits (or losses). Ingworth Church has an hourglass used for timing sermons, it's not known if it's still in use!

Aylsham

 The Aylsham Navigation brought prosperity to the town. Goods no longer had to come in by sea at Cromer or be transferred to wagons at Coltishall. The Great Eastern Railway Company (GER) came to Aylsham in 1880 and ran between Aylsham South and Wroxham. A rival company, The Eastern and Midlands, subsequently the Midland and Great Northern Railway (M&GN), set up shop in 1883 from Aylsham North. Today the only rail traffic running between Aylsham and Wroxham is the 15" narrow gauge Bure Valley Railway line (1990) with a footpath and cycle track running alongside. The churchyard contains the grave of landscape designer Humphry Repton.

Aylsham Millgate

The word gate here is used to mean street or way. Beccles on the River Waveney has several 'gates' too, for example Smallgate and Northgate. With the creation of the Aylsham Navigation, boats were able to work through five locks from the river at Coltishall to The Staithe at Millgate. The trade continued until 1912 when disastrous floods swept away some of the lock gates. The canal was formally abandoned in 1928.

The Mill at Burgh next Aylsham

Here the river was bypassed and a channel dug to accommodate Burgh Lock, part of the Aylsham Navigation.

Oxnead and Brampton

There's evidence (pottery shards) that the Romans were here but Oxnead's best known residents were the Pastons. The Paston Letters, written by members of a prominent fifteenth century Norfolk family, give an early picture both of domestic life and state matters. The house became a ruin after they left and what remains are the servants' quarters with nineteenth century additions.

Lamas looking north

Lamas, probably which means a loam marsh, was called 'Lamers' in the Domesday Book. Anna Sewell, author of *Black Beauty*, is buried in the graveyard of the former chapel here, and in the church there's a memorial window dedicated to Norfolk historian Walter Rye.

Buxton Mill and village

Buxton watermill, in common with many others in the Bure, Wensum and Yare valleys, was mentioned in the Domesday Book so there has been a mill on this site since at least 1086. The mill was last rebuilt in 1754. In 1933 the derelict lock on the Aylsham Navigation was filled in to make a road from Buxton to Lamas. In the church of St Andrew's (centre) there is a 1773 touching memorial to the child Mary Kent. The inscription reads "who died under 'innoculation'. Her fond parents, deluded by prevalent custom, suffered the rough officious hand of Art to aid the flourishing root of nature".

Horstead Lock

The first lock on the Aylsham Navigation was used for the first time March 16 1775 when the boat *Crampus* worked through, this was followed three days later by a Yarmouth keel with a cargo of bricks, pavements, coal, cinders and salt. The Navigation continued until the torrential rain in August 1912 swept away lock gates further up river and the system became unusable. A navigation is the term for a canalised river.

Coltishall

This picture represents so much change! Once part of the busy Aylsham Navigation, the river now ceases to be navigable (except for canoes and very small boats which can be ported round the lock). The disused lock has a sluice, used in flood prevention. *Ella* the last ever trading wherry was built here at Allen's Yard in 1912 and now lies derelict at the entrance to Decoy Broad. Wherries, with rare exceptions, have disappeared, but Coltishall Common is a popular cruiser mooring spot, especially with two pubs only a few yards away. The closure of RAF Coltishall in 2006 was a sad day for many. It had been an operational airfield since 1938. Douglas Bader was stationed here during the Second World War. Now its future is uncertain.

Belaugh Broad

Trolling along the river who would guess that this cut-off broad existed a short distance beyond the trees! This is a sight possible to see only from the air. It was mud-pumped several years ago to improve water quality.

The Capital of The Broads – Wroxham

The Broads boat hire industry began in 1878 when boat builder John Loynes diversified into hiring out boats from his Wroxham Yard. The 'World's Largest Village Store' – Roys of Wroxham set up shop here only a few years later. The store is actually across the river in Hoveton but 'Roys of Hoveton' doesn't have the same alliterative charm.

The Bure flows between Wroxham and Hoveton, past Wroxham Broad and Hoveton Great Broad. Hoveton Great Broad is not open to navigation but has a Nature Trail accessible only from the river. Salhouse Broad is opposite Hoveton Great Broad. Hoveton Little Broad is far left of picture.

Wroxham 1965

Two wherries are moored alongside the boatyards. Several boat-sheds occupy what will become valuable development land. Note the steepness of Wroxham Bridge.

Wroxham 2007

Several of the boatyards have gone, replaced often by houses. Roys Department Store has expanded and the number of dwellings in Hoveton has increased considerably. The green area to the right is the playing field of the new school next to the church along the Horning and Ludham road.

Wroxham Broad

The Battle for Black Horse Broad (aka Hoveton Little Broad)

This tranquil picture gives no clue to the arguments and wrangling concerning the Broad in 1949. Whilst the landowner wanted to put a chain across the entrance to keep out the public, a strong body of opinion within the Broads Preservation Society led by boat builder Herbert Woods fought the case.

From the *Daily Express* 12 March 1949

A landing craft with thirty men aboard invaded last night a stretch of the Norfolk Broads claimed as private. Stakes and chains guarding the entrance were pulled up with a winch. The expedition cost £60. The invaders, under Mr Herbert Woods – leader of a movement which claims all broads should be open to the public – were met by a policeman, an agent and a solicitor in rowing boats. The policeman took names.

The vision of the local policeman 'taking names' gives a comedic slant to the situation. However the deadly serious and important act was followed by the time-honoured solution – a compromise. The 'friendly agreement' (Herbert Woods' words) allowed the public into Black Horse Broad from the Saturday immediately before Easter Sunday until the second Saturday in September. Nowadays the Broad is open for Easter Week then from the late May Bank Holiday until the end of September.

Horning in October

Opposite: **Horning**

The coming of the boat hire industry and the interest in leisure pursuits at the turn of the last century put Horning 'on the map'. But there had been a foot ferry across the Bure for centuries (near picture at the first river bend). The Ferry Inn was bombed in 1940 and twenty people were killed. Stretches of river have acquired quaint names over the years but none more so than 'Cinder Oven Reach' which immediately precedes the entrance to Black Horse Broad (top left). It's a reminder of the coking oven in which coal was rendered into a smokeless fuel used in the maltings which once stood here.

Malthouse Broads and Ranworth

A view *almost* as good as this can be had by climbing the steep winding stairs to the top of Ranworth Church Tower, and to aid recovery there's a great Tea Shop in the churchyard (open in the season). Seen here are cruisers motoring along Ranworth Dyke to rejoin the River Bure. Ranworth Broad (entrance right) is closed to boats except for the ferry *Helen of Ranworth* which plies between Malthouse and Ranworth Broads taking visitors to Norfolk Wildlife Trust's thatched and floating Information Centre. From the upstairs windows of the centre can be seen rotted skeletons of abandoned wherries. It was here that in 1981 Vincent and Linda Pargeter recovered the hulk of the now restored wherry *Maud* which had been used first as bank reinforcement then filled with mud for a duck nesting site. In addition to the ferry there's a boardwalk from Ranworth village to the Information Centre.

Malthouse Staithe

St Benet's looking up river

Flood alleviation work is taking place at many locations in the Broads' network. The emphasis is on alleviation rather than on flood prevention which might be impossible to achieve. Considerable work is being undertaken here and at the mouth of the River Ant. In this picture the soke (sock) dyke parallel to the Fleet Dyke leading to South Walsham Broad (opposite side of the river to St Benet's) has been enlarged to accommodate increased flood water. The area of reed and scrub to the right of the Fleet Dyke is Ward Marsh. The shallow pool between the Abbey Gatehouse and the river has been filled in using dredging spoil. The Gatehouse is all that remains of a huge complex of monastic buildings whose footings are evident in the grass.

South Walsham Fleet Dyke 2004
Before the recent flood alleviation work began.

South Walsham Fleet Dyke 2007
The Fleet Dyke is yet another example of man's intervention in the Broadland landscape. Previously the river ran in a circuitous route round Ward Marsh (right of picture). A channel exists still round the edge of the marsh but it's unnavigable.

Reedcutting alongside the Fleet Dyke

Reed is cut in the winter months when the stems have turned a yellowy-brown and the seed heads are purple/brown. Reed cutting is mechanised today except for the areas where a motor scythe cannot reach. But even with modern machinery the reed cutter has his feet in icy water.

South Walsham Broad

This late evening picture shows most motor cruisers moored or mud-weighted for the night. Off to the right is the inner broad where access is allowed but mooring not permitted. Fairhaven Gardens, noted especially for their drum head primulas in the Spring, but beautiful at any season, run down to the inner broad.

The River Bure at Thurne Mouth

The massive amount of flood alleviation work undertaken in the last two years is well demonstrated here along the banks of the Bure. The Norfolk Wildlife Trust's Reserve is to the left of picture. The Thurne is bottom right.

Upton and the Bure

The cleared area visible above Upton Broad is a result of major scrub clearance effort during the winter of 2005/6. It was the Norfolk Wildlife Trust's last work under the Lottery Project. The purpose was to restore fen vegetation but the green triangle was left because it contains mature alder and oak. It's important to restore fen vegetation to provide habitats for wildlife such as swallowtail butterflies and bittern. The two pools are Upton Broad and Upton Little Broad. Only a dyke connects them today. In 2004 the Norfolk Wildlife Trust launched successfully a public appeal to buy two hundred and fifty acres of fen and wet woodland which included Upton Great and Upton Little Broads. Thurne Mouth can be seen downriver of Thurne Dyke and Thurne Mill (top right).

Acle Bridge

This is at least the third bridge across the Bure at this site and is the only river crossing on the Bure between Wroxham and Great Yarmouth. The original bridge was called Acle Wey Bridge – 'wey' is Old English for 'crossing'. There's reputed to have been the occasional hanging from its arches. This third bridge replaces a concrete one built in the 1930s which could not withstand the increased volume of traffic. This latest one was built in 1997 and cost £1.6 million.

Overhead Acle looking east

Once the area was a huge estuary. As water levels fell the River Bure emerged but it flowed into the North Sea north of Yarmouth. Now it joins the Yare before they flow under the Haven Bridge and out to sea. To drain the marshes there were a great many windpumps whose sails drove scoop wheels or 'turbines', a job now carried out by mechanical pumps. The notorious 'Acle Straight' (A47) starts here and runs in straight line (except for one bend) all the way to Great Yarmouth. Having single carriageways in both directions it has claimed countless lives and will continue to do so until it is dualled or an alternate satisfactory solution is found. Road traffic is expected to increase considerably when the new Yarmouth Outer Harbour is completed. The railway line from Yarmouth to Acle and Norwich runs parallel to the road. On the horizon lies the Scroby Sands windfarm.

Stokesby, looking south east

The Ferry Inn Stokesby is all the evidence that remains of a ferry across the river taking cattle to the opposite marshes. Parallel to the A47 road runs the railway line between Yarmouth and Norwich via Acle and veering off at an angle is the Yarmouth to Norwich line via Reedham. Remarkably both lines remain open today.

Ancient and Modern

The wind turbines on Scroby Sands off Great Yarmouth provide energy fed into the National Grid. The windfarm came on line in 2004 and can provide power for 40,000 homes. The marsh mills generated energy by wind power too but their job was to pump water from the marsh dykes into the rivers. In the foreground is Runham Swim Mill, cattle were made to swim across the river to graze the marshes. On the opposite bank is Perry's Mill (built between 1795 and 1825) – it is common for mills to have assumed the name of a one-time owner. Five Mile House Mill (1849) standing over 39 feet high is downriver of Perry's. The mills built after 1825 tended to be higher than the earlier ones. The five miles refers to the distance from Yarmouth's Haven Bridge. The mill furthest downriver (with restored sails) is Mautby Marsh Mill, originally eighteenth century but with later alterations. It has been converted to a house and the sails are tied.

Bure Loop

Here's an exciting project which might just happen in the fullness of time. The proposal is to excavate the land and produce a new expanse of water as a refuge for overwintering waders and other wildlife and possibly provide an area for water sports. The extracted spoil would be used elsewhere for flood alleviation. In order to achieve this the various agencies involved which include Norfolk County Council, English Nature, Sport England and BESL (Broadland Environmental Services Ltd) are dependent on Lottery Funding. The land, largely containing fields of oilseed rape in flower when this picture was taken, is contained by a rather dull stretch of the Bure to the left and by Breydon Water to the right.

The mouth of the Bure

The River Bure flows into Yarmouth Harbour between Breydon Bridge (right of picture) and the Haven Bridge (off picture to the left). By boat the last few hundred yards are a bit tricky and it's important to get the tide just right. Hire craft are not allowed left beyond this point. The Southern Rivers (the Waveney and the Yare) are reached by turning right and traversing Breydon Water.

Great Yarmouth looking south
Great Yarmouth's North and South Quays have a long history of trade, but all that might change when the new harbour is built at the South Denes.

RIVER ANT

Both the Bure and its tributary the Ant were canalised near to their sources. The North Walsham and Dilham Canal was created in 1825 and cargoes were carried by small specially built wherries. From the start the canal was not a great success because the North Walsham merchants preferred to land cargoes on the coast at Mundesley or Bacton and bring coal etc by road to North Walsham. A number of small 'market' wherries carried vegetables and their growers from the various staithes along the canal to Great Yarmouth markets. Traffic on the canal had dwindled for years, the last cargo carried was in 1934 coincidentally by the last trading wherry ever built, the *Ella*. At just over eight miles in length the Ant is one of the shorter Broadland rivers and the one most altered by man.

Antingham Ponds
The River Ant takes its name from two lakes at Antingham from which it rises. Antingham takes its name from the Norseman Anta whose ham or settlement was here.

North Walsham

North Walsham, in the middle of a mediaeval prosperous woollen producing area, gave its name to a type of lightweight woollen cloth as did its neighbour Worstead. The curving line (foreground left) is the route taken by the M&GN railway between Felmingham and North Walsham, it's now part of the Weavers Way long distance (56 miles) footpath which runs between Cromer and Great Yarmouth.

Briggate (or Bridge gate)

Briggate Lock is hidden in the trees at the point where the road crosses over it.

Ebridge Mill

The mill on the Dilham and North Walsham Canal was opened in 1826 to produce flour. Subsequently the provender mill (which closed in 1998) was built alongside and produced animal feed. Ebridge (derelict) Lock is to the right of the lower building.

Briggate lock and mill

The navigation ended here in 1935. In 1972 the mill was badly damaged by fire.

Honing looking up river

The navigation was popular with leisure sailors when W.A. Dutt wrote his book *The Norfolk Broads* in 1903. He says 'Dilham, with its lock and bridge, and Honing with its leafy long lane leading to the church, are among the pretty villages which a cruiser on the Upper Ant can visit'

East Ruston

Honing Broad lies somewhere between Honing and East Ruston. Long extinct, it was last shown on a map of 1730. Peat had been extracted here from the Middle Ages at least until the turn of the nineteenth century and a recent fire on East Ruston common ignited much of the brushwood thereby revealing the underlying peat baulks.

Dilham Dyke

A dyke (also known as Tyler's Cut) was dug out from the main navigation to provide access for market wherries up to Dilham village. It is navigable by small boats even today having been dredged regularly. There's a turning basin at Brick Kiln Bridge.

Hunsett Mill

Mr Hunn with his eel sett once lived here. The mill was built around 1860 to drain the marshes, a job now done by the pump house at the end of the dyke. In the 1970s the garden in summer was a riot of annual flowers and on at least one occasion an elderly lady was spotted wielding dustpan and brush collecting up stray petals.

Wayford Bridge

The A149 from Great Yarmouth to North Walsham carries traffic over the River Ant where originally there had been a ford. In Roman times there was a road from the west crossing at this point to reach Caister. Clearance under the bridge is only seven feet at high water, making it the end of navigation for many boats. In the distance stands Hunsett Mill.

Stalham Hire Cruisers

Does this colourful scene signify the end of the season, or the decline of the Boat Hire industry?

Stalham

Today this small market town is bypassed by the busy A149 built on the M&GN railway line which until 1959 ran from Great Yarmouth to Melton Constable and beyond. In the foreground stands Stalham Dyke leading from which (to the right) is The Poor's Staithe. The Museum of The Broads is sited here in former warehouse buildings. Wherries used to work up to Burton's Mill which stood at the end of Stalham Dyke.

Sutton Broad

Reeds encroach on any Broadland waterway not regularly cleared or used frequently. Sutton Broad used to occupy the whole of the valley bottom. Sutton Staithe has moorings at its end but the water all along the channel is shallow. Gone before World War One, a pioneering Freshwater Laboratory was founded here on the broad by members of the Gurney family. Their resources came from Gurneys Bank, later Barclays. The triangular area mid stream is a 'heater piece' so called because it takes its shape from an old fashioned flat iron.

Sutton Staithe

Barton Middle Marsh

Another heater piece exists where the river (right) flows down to Barton Broad whilst the channel to the left goes to Barton Turf Staithe.

Barton Broad in December

All evidence of summer activities has gone, the Norfolk Punt Club floating platform and *The Ark,* belonging to The Nancy Oldfield Trust, have been towed away. The cruisers are tied up elsewhere. After decades of erosion Pleasure Hill (the island mid broad) is being built up with coir mats planted with reed round the edge of the island.

How Hill

How Hill House is surrounded by some of the most attractive countryside in Broadland. The house, roughly in the 'Arts & Crafts' style of the period, was built in 1903 by architect Edward Boardman as his family home. The house looks out over the marshes to the recently restored Turf Fen drainage mill. There's another mill in the picture on the higher ground to the right, almost hidden by the trees. This mill was built in 1825 by the Ludham millwrights, the England family, for grinding corn. Boardman's Broad (to the right of picture foreground) was created along with its surrounding garden by Edward Boardman's grandson, Peter, thirty years ago. It's spring fed and has no access to the river.

The Bittern Project

Forty-two hectares of formerly arable land in the Ant valley have been purchased with European funding and are in the process of being restored to marsh to encourage the return of the bittern. There are now ten breeding pairs in Norfolk where once there was danger of extinction. The Broads Authority together with Wildlife Trusts, Natural England, the RSPB and other concerned parties are masterminding the project. Work involves the creation of extra reed beds, making dykes more wildlife friendly and the digging out of six shallow lagoons stocked with fish from the dykes. The new Buttle Marsh takes its name from a dialect noun for the bittern.

Ludham Bridge

A ford predated a bridge across the river here. Built in the 1930s this present bridge gives consternation to boaters passing *under* and amusement to those standing *on* the bridge because the approach has bends in either direction and it's impossible to see waterborne oncoming traffic until the last moment.

Ant mouth

Here the Ant joins the Bure but centuries earlier the course of the Ant flowed along the Hundred Dyke below Ludham Bridge eastwards to the Thurne. It's not uncommon for Broadland rivers to have altered course either naturally or by deliberation over the centuries. Traces of the causeway which ran parallel to the river from St Benet's to St James's Hospital and monastic chapel near Horning can be picked out. Ongoing flood alleviation work has been undertaken here too.

RIVER THURNE

The River Thurne leads to some of the best sailing on The Broads. Horsey Mere along Meadow Dyke and Hickling Broad, with its variety of watersports on offer, is accessible only to smaller craft for much of the season, and on occasions in the winter the water levels are so high that there is no gap at all under Potter Heigham bridge. Unless very familiar with the river it's a good idea to use the Bridge Pilot (mandatory for hire craft). At Hickling Staithe all the comforts of modern life (pub, shop, toilets) can be enjoyed, plus the facility to hire a bike and explore this quiet and interesting area at a leisured pace.

Thurne Mouth

Today the River Thurne (top of picture) flows south-west and joins the Bure but centuries ago it flowed in the opposite direction into the North Sea near Horsey. It's thought that at one time the upper Bure (mid picture left) approaching Thurne Mouth and the Thurne itself were all one river. There are examples all over Broadland where rivers have changed course either naturally or more commonly through man's intervention but even by Broadland standards a complete flow reversal is unusual!

Thurne Dyke looking towards Potter Heigham and the coast

The mill foreground is St Benet's Level Mill, so called because traditionally marshes were divided into drainage levels and St Benet's Abbey lies on the same marshes off picture to the left. The mill was restored (sails, cap and fantail reinstated, although the marshes in common with all others are now drained by a modern pump) by the Crown Commission in 1996 . The building with the green roof (right of the mill) is a First World War army hut subsequently used as a holiday home. Thurne Mill, also known as Morse's Mill, is at the entrance to Thurne Dyke. It's possible still to see the scar high up on the brickwork where during a gale in 1919 the brake wheel smashed through the brickwork when the cap blew off.

Womack Water

Leading from the Thurne and up into Ludham Village this stretch of water contains much recent history. Restored trading wherry 'Albion's' winter quarters are here. Here too is the base of the famous Hunter Fleet of traditional wooden sailing boats which in the summer are a glorious sight especially on the Thurne and Ant. An example of the recent flood alleviation work is the wide dyke to the left.

Ludham village

Ludham remains a model Broadland village, clustered round a central cross roads and with most of its services intact (surgery, butcher, village shop and post office, garage, pub, church). There's a pleasant short stroll from Womack Water (centre) into the village enabling boaters to top up their supplies.

Potter Heigham boatyard 1967

In the 1960s the renting out of hire cruisers was probably at its peak and Herbert Woods' yard (centre complex) was to the fore. The yard had also a long tradition of boatbuilding including the construction of airborne lifeboats during the Second World War (one is on view in the Museum of The Broads at Stalham). Coincidentally the Museum began its life here in the large shed (foreground) before moving to drier premises – flooding was commonplace on this site. The tall landmark 'Broads Haven' tower, at one time Herbert Woods' office, looks fairly squat in the picture but it's a dominant feature in the village. Woods' yard is famous among the sailing fraternity for the building and hiring out of the 'Lady' yacht classes (Perfect Lady and Leading Lady). Woods' motor cruisers included the 'light' classes (Leading Light, Queen of Light etc). The dykes were cut out from marshland by Herbert Woods in the 1920s.

Potter Heigham boatyard today

Many more boats tied up, and where have all the sailing cruisers gone?

Potter Heigham village

The usual views of Potter are of the quaint old bridge or the complex of Herbert Woods' Broads Haven boatyard, but here is the sad story of 'progress'. The village is divided now by the busy A149 Yarmouth to Great Walsham road built on the former railway line. When the railway ran through Potter, and the village had a station, at least it benefited the whole village, now it's a nightmare to cross on foot. Hickling Broad is in the distance.

Hickling Broad

This is the largest expanse of open water on The Broads. The Broad itself (top) measures approximately 346 acres of open water today compared with 196 acres shown on the Tithe Award map of 1840. The areas leading to the broad have picturesque names, Heigham Sounds, Duck Broad, Swim Coots, Rush Hill, Deep Dyke. During the First World War sea planes landed on the Broad; it was a bad weather alternative to the Royal Naval Air Station on the South Denes at Great Yarmouth. Many of the sequences for the 1952 film 'Conflict of Wings' were shot on Hickling Broad.

Hickling Heath

The only public road access is at this north-west end of the broad. The Pleasure Boat Inn with its narrow Hickling Staithe attracts water borne patrons and much fun can be had watching a large cruiser attempting to turn in a width shorter than the boat's length! The eight storeyed tower mill was built in 1818 and though used mainly for grinding wheat with its three pairs of stones, it had an auxiliary oat crusher.

Norfolk dinghies racing on Hickling

Martham Ferry

The ferry gives access to the National Trust's marshes at Heigham Holmes. The floating platform is pulled round into place by a chain on the opposite bank but the sight of a vehicle crossing beggars belief. The ferry is actually a seesaw! The vehicle travels across on the platform which is angled about four feet above horizontal. When the ferry reaches the opposite bank the vehicle moves forward slowly and the platform tips down gently until it touches ground again. A clever way of dealing with rises and falls of water level.

Martham Broad

Much of the Broad is now silted up as the abundant reed growth testifies. It's now part of a National Nature Reserve and managed by the Norfolk Wildlife Trust. The marsh harrier and bearded tit are among the species to be found here along with the swallowtail butterfly. Whilst most Broads were formed mainly from peat extraction, Martham is unusual because here in the Middle Ages clay for bricks was extracted. In the nineteenth century the Martham brickworks sent many wherry loads of bricks downriver for the development of the seaside town of Great Yarmouth. Boats pass through a narrow channel (mid picture) which leads to the end of navigation at Somerton Staithe. It's a very beautiful and remote area, but not quite as remote as one might think, making our way along the channel on a still bright morning with only ducks for company we came upon a lone canoeist pulled into the reeds having an animated conversation on his mobile phone! The original route of the river shows as a wavy line (foreground). This is the Hundred Stream denoting the mediaeval administrative boundary of West Flegg and Happing Hundreds (several different Hundred Streams or Rivers exist). Originally this Hundred Stream carried the waters of the Thurne out to sea near Horsey.

Somerton

The Somerton wind turbines were installed in 1992. They're thirty metres tall and have a life expectancy of twenty-five years. A higher one was added a few years ago despite local opposition. The Somerton turbines are dwarfed by the sixty-metre high ones out at sea on Scroby Sands which were installed in 2004.

Meadow Dyke

Sailing or motoring slowly along Meadow Dyke from Horsey Mere (off picture) into Hickling Broad (right) or through Heigham Sounds (left) and back into the River Thurne, the rest of the world seems miles away

Horsey Mere

This winter shot (not a boat in sight) demonstrates the area's vulnerability from a North Sea surge and in the 1953 floods thousands of acres went under salt water. Both Horsey and Hickling tend to be quieter because the larger boats cannot pass under the mediaeval Potter Heigham bridge unless the water level is very low. Some are too wide or too high whatever the height of the water. 'Horsey' is a corruption of 'Horse Island' and this area was an island when water levels were lower some centuries ago. Entry to the Mere is from Meadow Dyke (foreground) only.

The disused Waxham Cut (mid picture left) is accessible only by canoes and small rowing boats today. The Cut, made around 1820 before roads were commonplace, ran for three miles to provide access to a local brickworks and other small industries as well as providing water run off for the land. William Dutt writing in 1903 found that the recently overgrown cut had been 'cromed' and 'bottom-fyed' (the weeds cleared out [cromed] and excess mud removed [bottomfyed], and that wherries were again working along its length. Before it is accessible today it certainly needs considerable bottomfying again. Horsey Mill is almost off picture (right).

Horsey Mill

One of the later mills, built in 1912. Although the sails, cap and fantail have been replaced the mill is no longer in working order, the marshes are drained by a pump housed in a shed alongside. The mill is kept open by the National Trust and fine views from the cap gallery at the top justify the climb.

RIVER YARE

When Norwich was a thriving industrial area large vessels worked along the Yare to the Wensum where they tied up in the heart of the city. It was not unusual to look across the marshes anywhere between Berney Arms and Whitlingham and see a large ship making its way through what looked from a distance like green fields. At 25 miles it is the second longest of the Broadland rivers. To regenerate the Southern Broads area and raise awareness of the charms of the Yare Valley, in 2005 a thirty-five mile route along the Yare was created. The 'Wherryman's Way' can be walked cycled, reached by train or river bus at certain places along the Way and all along the route are markers outlining special features of that particular place. There are life-sized carved figures, audio posts, information boards and sculptures, all aimed to add to the enjoyment of the route.

Calveley Hall, Reymerston
Several very small streams meet east of here and become the River Yare which is known also as 'The Norwich River' – although it touches Norwich only on the city's eastern edge.

Barnham Broom

The village today has more associations with the leisure industry than with rural life. A golf course together with holiday and function accommodation attract visitors from further afield.

Marlingford Mill looking up river

A road has replaced the ford across the Yare at Marlingford. The mill (top right) was refurbished in 1850 but milling finished in 1912 because of damage caused by the great flood.

Bawburgh

The river flows under the busy A47 trunk road.

Bawburgh Mill

The mill ceased working in 1967 and has been converted to living accommodation. The appearance of the large number of small windows when lights are on in the evenings has been likened to an Advent Calendar!

Opposite: **Bowthorpe, river in flood**
The picture illustrates well the advisability of building above the flood plain.

UEA looking downriver

The stepped back living accommodation is an interesting departure from the usual rectangular of institutional buildings. The campus, designed by Denys Lasdun, (the first students were admitted in 1964) has a modern and exciting feel to it although there are many concrete walls which to some might appear stark, although its appearance has mellowed over the last forty years.

Looking upriver between Cringleford and Eaton

Flowing gently through Norwich's southern suburbs there's no indication that this gentle stream further downriver will become what used to be the most commercially important waterway in The Broads.

The Trowse Mill development looking upstream

Apart from the high volume of traffic on the road spanning the Yare there's no clue to the fact that the heart of the city of Norwich is less than a mile away.

Opposite: **Keswick Mill**

There's been a mill on this site since the thirteenth century. Its function was to grind corn and latterly to produce animal feedstuffs. It ceased working in 1976 and, like so many other watermills, has been converted into living accommodation. Watermills, because of their rectangular shape, lend themselves better to house conversion than do round tower windmills, however there are plenty of the latter in Broadland. The railway is the Norwich to Ely line.

Thorpe River Green

The bridge at this end of Harts Island is the scene of one of the worst railway crashes. On 10 September 1874 the mail train from Great Yarmouth collided head on with the express train from London and Norwich on the Great Eastern Railway's single track. The London train had been allowed to leave Thorpe Station before the arrival of the train from Yarmouth. Twenty-five people including both engine drivers and firemen were killed. A nearby pub was commandeered as a mortuary. Two of the railwaymen were buried in Norwich's Rosary cemetery, their headstones bearing relief carvings of railway engines.

Opposite: **Whitlingham Country Park**

Just upriver of this scene is the meeting of the Rivers Yare and Wensum which drops its name to become the Yare. The lakes were formed when gravel was excavated for the building of Norwich's Southern bypass. Here it's possible for anyone to cycle (there's a track right round the perimeter), to sail and learn to sail, canoe, row and windsurf. Picnics can be eaten and dogs walked. Whitlingham Country Park is a magnificent achievement and serves as Norwich's 'green lung'. To the left is Harts Island which was formed when a new cut was made so that wherries didn't have to lower their masts to pass under two railway bridges.

Urban sprawl and industry

Broadland Business Park at Thorpe, to the right, and a new housing development top left. The river widens considerably after its confluence with the Wensum. All boat traffic visiting Norwich comes along here just as sea-going ships did, but they brought cargoes of coal, grain and timber into the city.

Postwick and Surlingham

When the river's in flood (as here) the water finds somewhere else to go!

Bramerton Woods End

On the stretch of grass in front of the pub stands a carved wooden, life-sized, figure. It's Billy Bluelight, real name William Cullen. Billy was slightly eccentric. He was a great runner and his favourite Sunday sport was to race the pleasure steamers along the Wensum and Yare around the turn of the last century. Allegedly he'd call out to the passengers "My name is Billy Bluelight, My age is forty-five, I hope to get to Carrow Bridge, Before the boat arrive." Broad Norfolk contains, among other quirks, a singular use of verb tenses. Billy's nickname gives away his espousal of the Temperance Movement – a bluelight was one who had signed the pledge. For a while in the 1990s there was a pub in Norwich called the 'Billy Bluelight' – tongue in cheek?

Surlingham Broad

River trips from Norwich often visit Surlingham Broad where, through the water in the roped off area, sunken wherries can be seen. The wherries were placed here in the 1930s to protect the navigation channel.

Wherry graveyard

When sail gave way to steam some wherries were converted to motors, but most became redundant and suffered the same fate as many narrow boats on the canals, they were sunk.

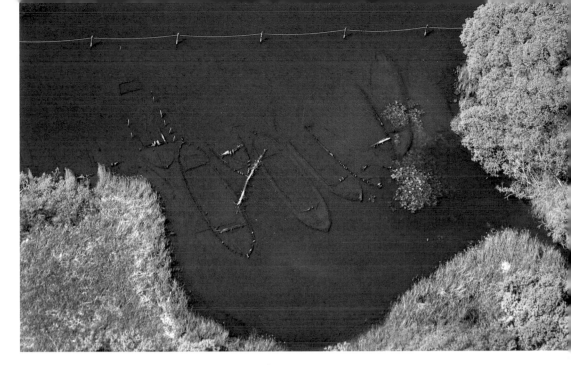

Brundall looking east

Brundall is a popular dormitory village for Norwich, well served by the railway lines running between Great Yarmouth, Norwich and Lowestoft. Low lying areas around the riverside are always at risk from flooding when tides are high.

79

Brundall 1960 and Brundall 2007

Brundall's growth began at the end of the last century when excursions from Norwich brought people by train or pleasure steamers from Great Yarmouth, carrying them to visit Brundall Pleasure Gardens. Compare the two pictures to see just how much expansion has taken place in the last forty years!

Coldham Hall

Until the 1960s it was possible to take a foot ferry across the river to Brundall. The pub on the left bank was the local of naturalist Ted Ellis who lived at nearby Wheatfen in Surlingham. Walter Rye writing his *Popular History of Norfolk* 1885 says of Coldham Hall 'A small red brick public house famous for Norwich Bean Feasts and Fishing Competitions'. A less happy event took place in 1774. Roy Clark in his *Black Sailed Traders* writes of a Norfolk Keel (forerunner to the wherry) which reached Coldham Hall in a very bad storm. The wind tore the single sail to shreds and trapped the skipper William Bell dragging him into the water where he drowned. As part of the Wherryman's Way route there is a life sized carved figure of a wherryman outside the pub.

Strumpshaw and Rockland looking up river

It was in the wide shallow lower valley of the River Yare that Dr Joyce Lambert (with others) was able to fathom out the origin of The Broads. Previously it had been thought that the great expanses of water were natural but by a series of soil borings into the river valley floor she discovered that broads' edges were vertical and the beds of the broads were flat and level (therefore man made) rather than sloping indicating a natural progression. It had been known for centuries that peat had been extracted from areas for fuel, there are receipts from St Benet's Abbey for supplies of peat to Norwich Cathedral as early as the eleventh century. But two and two were not put together until the 1950s which in itself seems extraordinary.

There are several men in their seventies walking around Norwich today who had been pupils at the City of Norwich School at the time and who had assisted her in obtaining samples of the river bed whilst working off a rowing boat in the middle of a broad. The tool used to obtain mud samples is now on display in The Museum of The Broads.

Rockland Broad

'The Fleet' and 'Short Dyke' run parallel into this very shallow Broad. Traditionally wildfowlers shot from gun punts here. The best known was 'Scientific' Fuller a marshman who lived in a houseboat on the broad and who shot everything that moved. He earned his living selling eels and wildfowl but shot rarer birds for collectors. The line of sallow cordoning off part of the broad marks the area where several wherries were sunk deliberately as war time defences. There was general concern in both World Wars that broads might be used to provide landing places for enemy aircraft. Hickling and Oulton Broad were two examples of locations where boats were sunk to prevent hostile flying boats from landing or where lines containing explosives were strung across the water.

Wheatfen

Much loved naturalist and writer Ted Ellis lived at Wheatfen. From 1928 until 1956 Ted was Keeper of Natural History at Norwich's Castle Museum. The estate is now a Nature Reserve run by a warden and by board members of The Ted Ellis Trust. Consisting mainly of marsh and fen and accessible to the public (some areas are open only at certain times of the year) the reserve contains walks, hides and information boards.

The Yare valley

The river, so quiet now, up to about fifty years ago was busy with commercial river traffic working between Great Yarmouth and Norwich. Part of the sugar beet processing factory is just visible (bottom right). The railway line Yarmouth to Norwich via Reedham runs alongside the factory although today the traffic (beet in, sugar products out) goes by road. Langley Dyke is upstream on the opposite bank.

Cantley village

The Reedham Ferry

Steam doesn't always give way to sail, these racing boats are going to have to manoeuvre round the ferry. This is the one remaining ferry across the Yare, until the 1940s it used also to be possible to be ferried across at Surlingham and Buckenham. The Reedham Ferry originally was hand wound but a motor was added to the previous craft in the 1950s. The present ferry was introduced in 1983. Two or three cars can be carried at a time or the occasional lorry returning from the Cantley factory. The river here has a tidal rise of about three feet. The ferry is propelled by chains across the river, the motor operates wheels which wind the pontoon along the chains. When the ferry is not under way the chains sit on the river bed.

Cantley Sugar Beet Factory

From the start of the 'campaign' in September until all the sugar beet has been processed in late winter a sickly sweet smell wafts across the marshes and can be picked up several miles away when the wind is in the right direction. This was the first of the series of modern beet processing factories in England, set up by a Dutchman in 1912. Today there are five factories, four of which are in Eastern England . Initially beet came in by river but the water is used now only in processing. Steam is billowing from the plant, not smoke!

Reedham

Reedham has witnessed more commercial river traffic than most Broads villages. First the keels and whatever preceded them, then the wherries sailing up to the numerous village staithes and to Norwich, lastly the big ships which towards the end of their period had to bump their way along the silted up river bottom all the way to Norwich. Cantley sugar beet factory initially used the river for transportation but in the last few years only the occasional oil tanker (mainly the tanker 'Blackheath') brought oil supplies in by water. Today road transportation is used all the time. Even when the New Cut (entrance bottom left of picture) was built traffic still joined the Yare at Reedham.

The New Cut

'Too late, too late' is the story of the New Cut. It was new in the 1830s and intended to provide a short cut into the River Yare at Reedham for boats entering the Broadland system via Lowestoft Harbour rather than via Great Yarmouth whose tolls were higher and whose harbour mouth silted up frequently. It was part of the Norwich and Lowestoft Navigation and the intention was to turn Norwich into a port. By 1847 however the railway had arrived and taken away all the trade.

Polkey's Mill at Seven Mile

Polkey's Mill is unusual in that the sails turn clockwise, the sails of the majority of broadland windmills turn anticlockwise. During restoration it was discovered that the original structure had re-used older material including that from a smock mill. The chimney to the right was part of the steam engine house, its height recently has been reduced on the grounds of safety. The machinery has been removed from the shed but inside there's an exhibition about 'The Land of Windmills' project of which this restoration was part. There's also a resident barn owl. The site is managed by the Norfolk Windmills Trust.

Flood Defence Scheme

The 'bluer' water is in the part of the Flood Alleviation Scheme where channels are dredged – often on either side of the river - to allow flooded rivers to overflow into a controlled space. The water has settled in the pools either side whereas in the river the mud is churned up by passing boats.

The route to the sea

Polkey's Mill is in the foreground, restored 2002–05 by millwright Vincent Pargeter. Cadge's Mill is downriver of Polkey's with Berney Arms Mill in the distance. Downriver on the opposite bank is Langley Detached Mill (detached from its parish, that is!) which is a Holiday Let.

Precarious position!

Setting back the bank and removing the existing piling on Reedham Marshes. Reed eventually will fringe the bank minimising erosion. Another part of the massive flood defence scheme.

Breydon Water

Here the waters of the Yare and Waveney meet and flow together through the wide expanse of Breydon, then under the Breydon and Haven bridges and out to sea at Great Yarmouth. Breydon means 'a broadening'. The dredged channel is to the right, and woe betide any straying boat which is left high and dry (until the next tide) on the mud. Arthur Patterson writing a century ago as 'John Knowlittle' wrote much about the wildlife here and it was a favourite haunt of wildfowlers and punt gunners. Berney Arms Mill (foreground), at a height of seventy feet six inches, was the tallest drainage mill in Broadland. There's a footpath along the north wall of Breydon from Great Yarmouth to Berney Arms Mill.

Early mist over Berney Marshes RSPB Reserve

Great Yarmouth harbour

The long seaward spit of sand of Yarmouth's South Denes has fallen into decline in recent years but the advent of the new harbour should breathe renewed life into the area. The inner harbour remains busy; supply ships servicing the North Sea gas rigs operate from here.

Opposite: **Work starts on the new Outer Harbour.**

RIVER CHET

In the 1950s the Chet was so overgrown that it was likened to Humphrey Bogart's river journey in the film 'African Queen'. Today there's an unencumbered if winding passage along the 3.5miles of river to the end of navigation at Loddon. Much work has been done recently on flood alleviation. At the river's entrance stands Hardley Cross, a monument marking the former change of jurisdiction over the river between the City of Norwich and borough of Great Yarmouth. That's now history.

The River Chet
Hardley Flood (top right of picture) stores the floodwaters of the River Chet and is a haven for wintering geese and wildfowl.

Loddon looking towards the sea

Loddon and Chedgrave

It's worth a special trip to Loddon just to see the magnificent church. There's a Latin inscription inside it which, translated, says, "Pray for the soul of James Hobart, Knight, who built this parish church of Loddon from the foundations at his own cost". There's also a riverside walk to Pye's Mill picnic area where an amusing set of carvings by Bungay woodcarver Mark Goldsworthy depicts a family shopping scene. Follow the carved figures and dropped shopping all the way into the town. Chedgrave can just be seen to the top right of picture. It is situated on the north bank of the river.

RIVER WENSUM

The upper reaches of the Wensum could equally be called 'The Land of Lakes'. The lakes have been created by the excavation of sand and gravel and today many of them are used for leisure activities such as fishing, landscape features on golf courses and wildlife refuges. Of all the seven rivers of Broadland, the Wensum provides the greatest contrast between its upper reaches and its mouth or, in the case of the Wensum, its confluence with the Yare. It rises in agricultural surroundings, flows through a large number of villages with watermills, and ends in the city of Norwich where, within living memory, sea-going ships tied up along what is now a complex of houses, flats, restaurants and shops. The only hint of Riverside's waterborne past is the Norwich Yacht station on one bank and derelict wharves on the other. But it's not only Norwich which has lost much of its industry. Paper making was a thriving business in the Swanton Morley area two hundred years ago. Paper and board were used in large quantities by the woollen industry for pressing, finishing, packing and wrapping. Among the skilled paper producers were the French Huguenots who had fled religious persecution; there was even a Huguenot church in Norwich. The printing paper for *The Times* was produced at Taverham in the mid nineteenth century, and paper was also made at Lyng and Bawburgh, Oxnead, Bungay and Norwich.

The source of the Wensum
This little stream, commercially so important in the city of Norwich from at least the eleventh century onwards, takes a circuitous path before it flows east and joins the River Yare. From its source between the hamlet of Oxwick and the fruit farms of Whissonsett it flows first south-west and then north-west towards Raynham Park.

The early Wensum at Raynham Park

Fakenham town centre

The church is hemmed in by other buildings. Although probably fourteenth century in origin it was given the usual Victorian facelift.

Opposite: **Fakenham looking north west**

The river (foreground) skirts the town to the south. Two unusual features for a Norfolk country town are the racecourse and the Museum of Gas. The racecourse has held National Hunt races since 1905. The Museum of Gas is located, not surprisingly, in the old gas works.

Fakenham Mill

Now converted to apartments the mill worked for about two hundred years from 1720. The watercourse was altered to obtain a sufficient dam. The mill was worked in conjunction with the next two upstream at Hempton and Sculthorpe as they had control of the water flow. In the early twentieth century it was converted to steam.

Looking up river to Pensthorpe

These former sand and gravel workings provide an ideal environment for hundreds of waterbirds and waders. Migratory birds visit in winter whilst over seventy different species breed here during spring and summer.

Sennowe Park, Guist

The grandson of the founder of the original travel agency, Thomas Cook, created an estate and model village here at Guist, his descendants live here still. In 1905 the lake was dug out using steam engines and with the help of a miniature railway.

Bintree Mill

The mill was used as the location for the 1996 production of *The Mill on the Floss*.

North Elmham Mill

The mill, powered by turbines, was producing animal feed as late as 1970. It was also known as Grint Mill.

The Blackwater river
The small Blackwater tributary (left) joins the Wensum.

Opposite: **Swanton Morley looking upriver**
The mill originally ground flour but in 1812 it was recorded as producing paper. The building was demolished around 1840 but *White's Norfolk* of 1845 records that one of the pubs was 'The Paper Makers Arms'. The flooded pits are now used for fishing.

Bylaugh Park

Architectural historian Nikolaus Pevsner writing in 1960 described Bylaugh Hall as 'a conspicuous ruin'. It has been restored recently. Bylaugh's architect was Charles Barry junior who built also the Great Eastern Hotel at Liverpool Street Station. His more famous father, also Charles Barry was, along with A.W.N. Pugin, the architect for the new House of Commons (the previous Palace of Westminster had been destroyed by fire in 1834).

Lenwade Mill

There had been a previous mill on the site but the present one was built in 1890 at a cost of £900. Latterly it produced animal feed, ceasing in 1984. After standing empty for some years this Grade II listed building has been converted sympathetically into housing. Parson Woodforde records in his diary that he sold corn to the Lenwade miller who would have worked the earlier mill.

Lenwade looking towards Lyng

The numerous lakes created by gravel extraction in the upper reaches of the Wensum did not appear until after the 1945–6 Popular Edition Survey Map was published so it's reasonable to assume they all have been dug since then to provide aggregate for road building and construction.

The Wensum at Ringland
If this is going to be an extension of the golf course then getting out of those sand bunkers is going to be a bit tricky!

Ringland

Ringland village nestles in the Wensum Valley but the nearby Ringland Hills straddle the forty metre (fifty two feet) contour meriting hill status indeed in Norfolk!

Hellesdon Mill and Costessey looking up river

There had been a mill on the site since Saxon times until the last one was destroyed by fire in 1924. At one time it ground rapeseed (Colza) oil for lamps. Colza oil was produced also at the mill built into the gatehouse of St Benet's Abbey. Hellesdon is in the foreground, Costessey is on the opposite side of the river.

Costessey looking upstream

Costessey ('Cossey') is now a suburb of Norwich. Old Costessey has a thirteenth century church. Costessey Brickworks produced the white bricks which are to be found in Norwich's Plantation Garden and a range of decorative bricks which adorn Victorian and Edwardian buildings (the former Royal Hotel for example) in Norwich and elsewhere.

New Mills

This mill, which is within the city walls, was new in the fifteenth century and used originally for grinding corn. The present building dates from the nineteenth century when it had a far less picturesque function – pumping sewage.

It has been standing empty for decades but the machinery is intact and it is hoped to preserve the building. Now surrounded by new housing some of which has river frontage, this is the end of navigation on the Wensum. The church is St Miles, Coslany, now used as a centre where children can learn about things scientific.

114

The city of Norwich

From a height of three thousand feet it's easy to see the embracing curve of the river. This explains why Norwich was such a good strategic place to found a city; stout flint walls were built to surround the part which didn't have river frontage. Today's inner ring road follows the same line. The artificial mound on which the castle stands is in the centre of the picture, with the turquoise elliptical roof of the new Forum building below it. To the right of the Forum, also with a turquoise roof, is the rectangle of the new Chapelfield Mall. Norwich's one remaining railway station, Thorpe, is in the top right quarter of the picture, with the green rectangle of Norwich City's football ground to its right. The other green rectangle, close to the cathedral, is the Norwich School (King Edward VI Grammar School) playing field. The New Mills of the previous picture straddles the river (bottom left quarter).

115

The heart of the city

A city of innumerable new apartments

Wherever an industrial building along the riverside is demolished (Read's Flour Mill, Boulton & Paul works, the Gasworks, warehouses, Carrow works) it seems that the site is redeveloped with apartment blocks. The exception is the shiny curved-roofed new swimming pool. In the foreground is Carrow road bridge with the recent Novi Sad (Norwich's Serbian twin town) foot-bridge upstream. Downstream of Carrow Bridge and on opposite banks stand two Boom Towers between which a chain could be fixed to keep out invaders. The confluence of the Wensum and Yare is less than a mile downriver.

116

Where the Wensum meets the Yare

The area known as Trowse Eye is scheduled for redevelopment. To the left is 'The Deal Ground' where part of the Colman's Mustard works stood. Here wooden crates were assembled from deal and used for packaging Colman products. Deal is from the Dutch 'deel' meaning a plank. On the opposite side of the river the former Norwich Power Station and Gas Works stood. It is a golden opportunity to create an impressive river approach into Norwich and consultations are ongoing today. Factors such as dealing with any soil contamination and building above the flood plain are having to be taken into consideration, together with the proposal for another river crossing.

RIVER WAVENEY

Each river valley has its own characteristics and the Waveney's landscape is predominantly one of drained marshes. Although considered 'harsher' than areas where fen and carr vegetation predominate (a carr is a fen woodland which has progressed from unmown fen, thus enabling small saplings to germinate) its wide open skies are magnificent.

The source at Redgrave Fen

The River Waveney and the River Little Ouse rise within a very short distance of one another. The Waveney flows eastwards to join the waters of the Yare in Breydon Water whilst the Little Ouse flows westwards to join the Great Ouse which flows out to sea at King's Lynn. But the Suffolk Wildlife Trust's Redgrave Fen is perhaps more famously known as a habitat of the rare raft spider, which probably doesn't care too much about what flows where. Redgrave Fen is the largest fen in lowland England.

Diss

The river, still a relatively small stream, skirts the southern edge of this small market town. More impressive is the Mere, six acres of open water with the town built round it, and reckoned to be sixty feet deep (mainly mud).

Hoxne Mill

Hoxne (pronounced hoxn) Mill when built in 1846 was powered by an undershot water wheel, subsequently converted to steam power, hence the tall chimney. Built to grind grain the mill at some time in its working life was converted temporarily to flax and linen production.

Opposite: **The Waveney Valley looking upstream**

Away from the river valley this is clearly an arable farming area. Billingford Mill (bottom right) was built in 1859 to grind corn. Shortly after it opened a bakehouse was erected within the site.

Harleston

A bypass now separates the higher ground on which the town was built from the river. A foundry in the town made a new iron waterwheel for Mendham Mill which had a huge capacity for milling having nine pairs of stones.

Needham

The brick and pantiled mill was built in 1870 following a fire which destroyed the previous one. It ceased working in 1934.

Mendham

Mendham Mill & Alfred Munnings 1878–1959

Alfred Munnings, son of the miller, was born at the mill. His paintings of horses and of gypsies brought him fame and fortune. He was apprenticed to a Norwich printer designing advertising posters but in his spare time he attended Norwich School of Art. His dedication repaid him handsomely and he became president of the Royal Academy.

The mill, built around 1820, produced flour which was taken to Bungay for transportation by wherry. It ceased milling in 1938.

Wortwell Mill

Eels favoured the water round the mill and eel catching was a lucrative sport for the miller. The mill stopped working in 1948.

Homersfield

An alternate name for Homersfield is St Mary South Elmham. 'The Saints' are a group of parishes whose chief characteristic is inaccessibility! Winding lanes with very old and beautiful houses abound. South Elmham contains eight parishes, for example: St Andrew South Elmham, St Peter South Elmham etc. whilst there are five parishes in the Ilketshall group: Ilketshall St Andrew (very confusing), Ilketshall St John, and so on. Homersfield, or rather St Mary South Elmham, is on the edge of 'The Saints'. Be sure to carry a map if you venture further into Saints Country. Homersfield has also the oldest surviving concrete bridge in England, built in 1909.

Bungay in winter

The straight road was built on the route of the old Waveney Valley railway line which ran from Beccles to Tivetshall Junction (to connect with the Norwich–London line). Bungay Golf Course has a magnificent site on the higher ground of Outney Common. The Common belongs to several owners all of whom have at least one 'going'. A 'going' entitles each owner to certain grazing rights.

Bungay

The Bigod family came over here with William the Conqueror. The castle was begun in 1070 by William de Noyers but soon taken over by Roger Bigod. Roger's son Hugh began the fortifications in 1165 and another Roger Bigod rebuilt the whole in 1294. It is now protected by a Castle Trust. St Mary's church tower dominates the landscape. This church is declared redundant but used for occasions such as concerts and the Remembrance Day service. In the churchyard are the remains of a Benedictine Nunnery. During a terrible storm in 1577 with the parishioners cowering in the church, a ferocious large black dog ran down the aisle attacking the congregation. He's a legend now but 'Shuck' known also as the Black Dog is commemorated with a plaque in the town centre. Sightings of 'Shuck' are common all over East Anglia and have associations with the Devil. The round tower of Holy Trinity church, now the parish church, has Saxon origins.

The town received a commercial boost with the canalisation of the river in the seventeenth century. Wherries were able to work through locks at Geldeston, Ellingham and Wainford to reach the heart of Bungay. The river describes a wide curve round the town. In the distance is the tall white silo tower of the former maltings at Wainford.

Wainford Mill

It's easy to visualise a wherry making its way upstream to Bungay, through Wainford Lock, which is hidden behind the silo and on the opposite side of the road. The locks were relatively spacious enabling larger wherries to reach Bungay.

Ellingham Mill

Ellingham Mill today is the home of an artist and more inspirational surroundings could hardly exist anywhere. The lock is just off picture to the right.

Geldeston floods

Beccles

The height of the churchyard above the road below can be judged by the size of the parked cars. It's easy to see why it was considered too risky to build the tower at the west end of the church since the churchyard is so small and so close to the edge of the cliff. Several of the alleyways from the higher ground to the lower are called 'scores' e.g. Railway Score. Lowestoft has an even larger number of scores running down to the sea shore. The road below the church is called 'Puddingmoor' – 'pudden' is a dialect word for a toad and being so close to the river would be a likely habitat for frogs and toads. A railway line used to span the river.

Beccles Quay

Now providing mooring for the many visitors who come to Beccles by water, the quay was once busy with boats bringing timber to the sawmills which stood where the row of new houses now stand. Steam packets once operated between Beccles and Great Yarmouth and, by 1833, there was a regular weekly service between London and Norwich run by the London, Lowestoft, Norwich and Beccles Shipping Company.

Beccles church

From the river the church stands high on a 'cliff' with the land falling away close to the west window and this is possibly the reason for the separate church tower, and for it to be sited at the eastern end. On occasion the tower is open and magnificent views across the marshes are to be had.

Flood defences downstream of Beccles

Mutford Lock

Here is one of the exits from The Broads into the North Sea, the other is at Great Yarmouth. The lock is unusual because of the complicated pattern of water movement. There are two tides arriving from opposite directions about an hour and a half apart with level water three-and-a-half hours later, hence the double set of lock gates. The tide from Lowestoft into Lake Lothing (left of picture) is the earlier, followed by the tidal effect from Great Yarmouth which arrives via Breydon Water, the River Waveney and Oulton Dyke.

Opposite: **Oulton Broad looking inland**

The keeper of Mutford Lock has to liaise with the signal box staff at the railway swing bridge so that tall-masted boats can pass through both.

Oulton Broad and out to sea

In order to create Lowestoft Harbour a channel was cut through the shingle bank from Lake Lothing to the sea in the early nineteenth century. The Lake is often referred to as 'the salt side' (of Mutford Lock). Ness Point is the most easterly part of Britain and on it stands the wind turbine nicknamed 'Gulliver'. Carlton Marshes (foreground right) are part of the Suffolk Wildlife Trust's Nature Reserve.

Oulton Dyke and the River Waveney

The straightening and deepening of Oulton Dyke had great commercial implications. Sea-going ships could then use it. By linking Lowestoft Harbour with the Broads' network, cargo-carrying boats were no longer dependent on Yarmouth Harbour which charged high dues and often silted up. And the advent of the New Cut in 1832 completed this quicker route for waterborne traffic bound for Norwich.

Somerleyton Staithe

The railway swing bridge was installed in 1847 and is still in use. It's part of the Lowestoft to Reedham and Norwich Line. Among the rail freight were bricks made at the nearby Somerleyton brickworks. The brickyard was sited where the mooring basin now stands. Wherries also transported bricks, some of which were used to build Liverpool Street Railway Station.

Somerleyton Hall

The Hall was built for Sir Samuel Morton Peto, who was knighted for building a railway to solve the supply crisis in the Crimean War. The Hall was begun in 1844 when Morton Peto was at his most successful as a railway and civil engineering contractor. His many building contracts included the installation of Nelson's Column and the Reform Club. He had railway interests in several countries including Argentina and Canada. He was a Member of Parliament and a guarantor for the Great Exhibition in 1851. He bought Lowestoft Harbour, ten years after the New Cut and Norwich and Lowestoft Navigation failed, and developed Lowestoft as a fishing and commercial port. The year after he was knighted (1855) it all went wrong. He was declared bankrupt and the Hall was sold to the Crossley family in whose hands (as Lord Somerleyton) the house remains.

Flooding at St Olaves November 2006

The River Waveney (top) and the New Cut (foreground) divide just off picture. The mill on the right hand bank of the Waveney is a hybrid between a trestle and a smock mill. The railway is the Lowestoft to Norwich line which runs parallel to the New Cut. In times of excessive flooding the line itself becomes under water. Haddiscoe Bridge spans the New Cut, St Olaves' Bridge spans the Waveney from Suffolk into Norfolk.

Opposite: **The confluence of the Waveney and the Yare**

The rivers meet at Burgh Castle (*Gariannonum*). All that is left of the Roman/Saxon Shore Fort is the rectangle of flint walls and circular bastions at the corners (left of picture on the Waveney). By the fifth century AD the Romans had departed and the fort began to disintegrate, later to be occupied by a monastic order. The navigation channels are clearly marked. The Turntide jetty at the confluence was put there in the 1830s to speed up the tidal flow through Breydon. If you're lucky you might, from a boat, see a seal or two basking on the jetty.

BIBLIOGRAPHY

Adderson R. & Kenworthy G., *Country Railway Routes – Melton Constable to Yarmouth Beach*. Middleton 2007

Clark Roy, *Black Sailed Traders*. David and Charles 1972

Dutt W. A., *The Norfolk Broads*. Methuen 1903

Dymond David, *The Norfolk Landscape*. Alistair Press 1990

Ellis E. A., *The Broads*. Collins 1965

Ekwall Eilert, *Oxford Dictionary of English Place Names*. OUP 1970

George Martin, *The Land Use, Ecology and Conservation of Broadland*. Packard 1992

Hamilton's Navigations. Hamilton 2001

Harrod Wilhelmine, *The Norfolk Guide*. Alistair Press 1998

King Clive, *The Trowse Triangle*. Norwich Rivers Heritage Group 2004

Linsell Stuart, *Hickling Broad and its Wildlife*. Terence Dalton 1990

Malster Robert, *The Norfolk and Suffolk Broads*. Phillimore 2003

Malster Robert, *Wherries and Waterways*. Terence Dalton 1971

Pevsner Nikolaus, *The Buildings of England*, 2 vols. Penguin 1976

Rye Walter, *History Of Norfolk*. Elliott Stock 1885

Wade Martins Susanna, *A History of Norfolk*. Phillimore 1988

White's Norfolk 1845. David & Charles reprint

Williamson Tom, *The Norfolk Broads – a landscape history*. Manchester University Press 1997